Aerial photograph showing Headcorn looking eastwards from the parish church, taken 17th August 1929. (Kent Messenger)

INTRODUCTION

The first recorded discovery of human occupation in Headcorn is a polished flint axe dating from c.2000-2500 BC, which was dredged from the School Stream behind Austen House in 1935 AD. It is uncertain when a permanent settlement was established at Headcorn, but certainly one existed by Saxon times, as is evidenced by its place-name. It probably began as one of the many dens, or clearings, named after their first owners, or the distant manors to which they were attached, in the Wealden Forest of Andred. According to the Oxford Dictionary of Place Names, 'Head' derives from the Old English personal name Huda, while 'corn' signifies a landslip or fallen tree. Thus the name Headcorn might mean 'Huda's fallen trees'.

Here then was one of the dens to which pigs were driven from the more populous northern regions of the county to feed on acorns. Even today maps of the area show a preponderance of north-east to south-west routes, indicating the lines of many ancient droveways. The main pattern is the same in the twentieth century as it was in the eighth. Various places had rights of pannage, as it was called, in different clearings and Headcorn was connected with the Faversham area in this way. The route (C258) starting at the White Horse cross-roads, and including King's Road and Lenham Road, is known as the 'Headcorn to Faversham road'. The earliest written record pertaining to Headcorn is the grant by King Offa in 791 AD of Southolmenden (Southernden) on the north-eastern boundary to Christ Church, Canterbury. Though Headcorn does not figure in the Domesday Book of 1086, the Domesday Monachorum, the ecclesiastical survey made at the same time, records the existence of a church at 'Hedekaruna', so plainly the Church's commissioners managed to penetrate the forest even if the King's men did not! The actual foundation of the parish as a unit of civil and ecclesiastical government dates from the appointment of Henry of Ospringe as the first Rector in 1222 by

The High Street looking east from the George and Dragon, taken in 1911 and showing the decorations across the road and on the shops. The occasion was the coronation of King George V. No. 37 High Street is Shersby's baker's shop.

The High Street looking west, 1910.

1

Henry III. However, in 1239 the king gave the den of Headcorn, with its rectorial endowments, to the Hospital of St Mary (known as the Maison Dieu) at Ospringe, near Faversham. In 1251 the master and brethren of Ospringe were granted a weekly market on Thursdays and an annual fair at Headcorn on SS Peter and Paul's Day, 29th June.

In 1482 the Hospital was dissolved when its only two remaining members left. In 1516 St John's College, Cambridge, was given the Maison Dieu properties by Henry VIII at the request of the Bishop of Rochester, John Fisher. The grant was renewed by the king four years later. The fair was later held on the 12th June, having apparently been merged with the Trinity-tide fair of Moddenden (Moatenden) Priory. The weaving industry was established here in the fourteenth century, during the reign of Edward III, and brought prosperity to the region, as is shown by a number of houses built at that time and the enlargement of the parish church.

Wat Tyler's rebellion of 1381 had, as one of its causes, jealousy and dislike of the prosperous clothiers. Among the leaders of the Kentish rebels was John Brise of Headcorn, while a Headcorn Boorman is said to have handed Tyler a stone to throw at the king. In 1450 some 80 men of Headcorn, including several Burdens, took part in Jack Cade's rebellion and received pardons. No doubt our oldest inhabitant, (if only it could speak) the Headcorn Oak, which stands near the south door of the church, would tell many a tale. The age of this venerable tree has been estimated to be anything up to 1200 years. However, Mr Alan Mitchell of the Forestry Commission has made a study of old oaks and compared his own measurements with those taken by Mr Robert Furley, F.S.A. in 1878. His conclusion is that the tree is about 500 years old.

The High Street looking east, 1906.

The High Street from Charles Brandley's Bakery, 1910.

The High Street in 1920. The motor van being loaded with bread is standing outside Mr A. Shersby's baker's shop. Mr Shersby had the last shop in Church Walk, where he made his bread and delivered it on a tricycle. After moving to the High Street he was the first Headcorn tradesman to have a motor van. This is now 37 High Street, a chemist's shop.

This illustration from an engraving shows the church before 1880.

HEADCORN PARISH CHURCH

There has been a church in Headcorn since at least the eleventh century, as is shown by the reference to Hedekaruna in the Domesday Monachorum, the ecclesiastical survey made at the time of the Domesday Book. The chancel of the present church of SS Peter and Paul is believed to mark the site of the nave of the eleventh century building, the oldest parts of the present church being the north and east walls of the chancel. Similarly, the Lady Chapel is thought to occupy the site of the twelfth century south aisle. The thirteenth century saw the construction of a new nave, about half the length of the present one, and possibly a cell on the site of the Vicar's vestry, which dates from the early fifteenth century. The nave was lengthened in the fourteenth century and the south aisle constructed in the early fifteenth. Late in the same century the tower and south porch were built.

Kent's Chantry was founded in the Lady Chapel in 1466 under licence granted by Edward IV to ' . . . Master Thomas Kent, Clerk of our Council, and to Robert Kent, Proctor General of the Court of Canterbury, to found, erect and establish a perpetual chantry of one perpetual chaplain, to celebrate Divine offices every day at the altar of the blessed Mary, in the parish church of Hedecrone . . . ' The room over the porch, which has a squint into the aisle, may have housed the chantry priest. The Lady Chapel is nowadays used for weekday services and the reservation of the Blessed Sacrament. The carved Bishop's chair, which stands in the sanctuary, was said, in 1878, to have come from Bristol Cathedral.

In the wall of the south aisle is an altar-tomb bearing the Culpeper arms, which are also to be seen over the west door. The font, dating from about 1450, is richly carved and octagonal in shape. At the west end of the aisle, near St Nicolas' Chapel, is the ancient parish chest. The chancel was formerly separated from the nave by a rood-screen, of which only the lower portion remains. Behind the pulpit are the blocked doorways of the rood-loft staircase. The present pulpit was constructed a hundred years ago from old panels found in the church. Its tester, however, formed part of the three-decker pulpit of 1790, which stood further west and is shown in one of the Society's photographs. The carved wooden lectern near the pulpit was given by the Baroness Burdett-Coutts in 1881.

Headcorn church looking west, showing traces of the old main road, taken in 1880.

Panoramic view from the church tower looking north to the White Mill, 1907.

On the floor nearby is a brass to a young boy, John Byrd, who was born on 10th May 1629 and died on 31st January 1636/7. It records that he '. . . delivered many godly exhortations to his parents takinge his leave of them with such unexpected expressions as are not common in so young a child . . .'

The nave roof, formed of massive rafters, is the greatest single glory of the church. The earliest reference to the bells is dated 1638. A record of work done in 1684 indicates that there were then five bells, but by 1766 there were eight. The present organ was built in 1922 and replaced an earlier one installed sometime after 1880. Before that there was a barrel organ and earlier still string and wind instruments were used. Two of the wind instruments are preserved in the vestry. The stained glass windows are mostly modern, though some ancient glass depicts St Thomas, St Laurence and the wheel of St Catherine. The modern glass commemorates Queen Victoria's Golden and Diamond Jubilees, the Burden/Borden family, Charles and Sarah Elizabeth Potter and Arthur Edward Stuart.

An interior view of Headcorn church, looking west, before 1900.

The parish church and 'old oak tree' from the south. The age of the oak is given as 1,008 years, though in the light of recent research this should not be taken too seriously. Date 1910.

Brass to John Byrd, 1636/7, in the parish church.

The Lady Chapel in Headcorn church at the rededication in 1905, following its restoration.

THE OTHER CHURCHES

BAPTIST CHURCH

The Baptist community in Headcorn dates from 1675. The first chapel occupied the site where Bounty Farm now stands in Love Lane, Rumpton. The graveyard still remains and has been recorded by the Local History Society. The present building in Station Road was opened in 1819, with the addition of a hall in 1971. It was further renovated and extended in 1978.

CHURCH OF ST THOMAS OF CANTERBURY

Having previously used the village hall, Headcorn's Roman Catholics acquired their own building in 1968, when the Church of St Thomas of Canterbury was erected in the grounds of Vine Cottage, 15 Station Road.

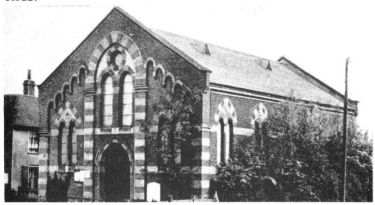

The Methodist Chapel (built in 1867) from the churchyard. Photograph taken 1910.

METHODIST CHURCH

The exact date of the first Methodist Society in Headcorn is not certain, but they built their first chapel for worship separate from the parish church in 1805. The present building cost £800 when it was put up in 1867. A Centenary Pageant was staged in July 1967.

The Old Vicarage 1910.

The Old Vicarage shortly after restoration in 1950.

The Baptist Chapel in 1910, built in 1819 to replace the meeting house in Love Lane, used since 1675. A graveyard remains in Love Lane, but the meeting house is now two cottages.

HEADCORN MANOR or THE OLD VICARAGE

This fine house, standing almost in the churchyard near to the west end of the church, represents the apex of domestic architecture in the fifteenth century. The building dates from around 1470 and, after restoration some years ago, the house has re-gained its original appearance; previously it had been divided into cottages. Technically this type of construction is a Wealden hall house: many others can be seen around Headcorn, but none are as perfect as this example. Chimneys were not used extensively in domestic houses until around 1520, the fire usually taking the form of a central hearth or brazier. The main room of a hall house was normally open up to the rafters, the smoke escaping through louvres in the roof. The blackened rafters of houses whose roof area has since been ceiled over, are a good indication that they are of mediaeval origin.

The name 'Headcorn Manor' is a misnomer, the manor house of Headcorn having been Rushford from the thirteenth century onwards. For many years it was known as the 'Old Vicarage' but, as there are other 'old vicarages' in the village, the house is most confusingly named. The upper storey overhangs at either end in a jetty, to the back as well as the front. It is a type of house known as a 'double wealden' and is quite rare. Other examples are to be seen at Iden Green, near Sandhurst, and at Pattenden in Goudhurst.

Jettying is not simply an aesthetic feature of timber-framed buildings, though it undoubtedly adds to their charm, but also has a structural significance. By projecting beyond the lower wall face, protection from the worst of the elements was afforded, particularly to the vulnerable foundations. The house stands on what was the original High Street, now identified by Church Walk and Gooseneck Lane.

The Old Vicarage in 1914, when it was divided into two cottages.

THE RIVERS AND BRIDGES

The River Beult rises in Goldwell, in Great Chart, and flows from east to west through the parish of Headcorn just south of the village, joining the river Medway below Yalding bridge. It has three tributaries: the River Sherway in the east with a north-easterly course; the Hammer Stream just west of the church, with a southerly course, and the School Stream, hardly more than a large ditch, which flows from the north-east and joins the Beult just east of the Hammer Stream.

The name Beult is of Scandinavian origin and means 'swollen belly'. This is very apt as the river regularly overflows its banks. Throughout the history of the village there are references to floods, the most disastrous being that of 6th January 1776, which was accompanied by a bad storm and caused much damage. Another occurred on 25th January 1809 when the river rose even higher. Mudding of the river (removal of silt by hand) was organised by the parish between 1825-1836 to provide work for soldiers who had returned from the war with France and had been unemployed for some time. Today, the Southern Water Authority controls the river, which has some interesting flora, and various angling clubs have fishing rights to certain stretches.

There are three road and three foot bridges crossing the River Beult with mediaeval origins. The road bridge at Hawkenbury is on the boundary with Staplehurst and only one pier is in Headcorn parish, which has been a bone of contention since the days of Edward I. The next bridge is to be found on the road to Frittenden. It is called Stephen's Bridge, after Archbishop Stephen Langton, who is thought to have had it built in the early thirteenth century to facilitate the journey from his manor house at Charing to Slindon, in Sussex, where he died in 1228. It is a beautifully proportioned stone structure consisting of two arches, with a recess in the centre which may be used as a seat or a place of refuge from the traffic. The third road bridge is on the road to Biddenden and Tenterden, now the A274. It was built in 1815, probably on the site of an earlier bridge, by French prisoners of war who were employed to construct the road from Gladwish Corner, Sutton Valence, to Bounds Cross, Biddenden.

On a footpath leading from Smarden Road to Headcorn aerodrome is a structure with mediaeval origins, though much restored, but about which little is known. Pell Bridge, which is reached along a footpath of Bethersden marble south of the church, also has mediaeval origins. The original piers can be seen when the water is low, but the bridge, originally of wood, has been rebuilt in metal in recent years. It is thought that this is the route the clothworkers would have taken with their laden packhorses to Cranbrook, one of the main cloth centres in the region. Another footpath at Place Farm leads over a bridge to Kelsham with traces of the mediaeval work just visible. By crossing first Stephen's Bridge, then the railway

Pell Bridge, 1916. Half of original timberwork visible on left-hand side.

Hawkenbury Bridge 1987.   (K.C. Boorman)

An etching by T.L. Burden of the bridge over School Stream at the foot of Mill Bank, 1900.

bridge and then turning towards Waterman Quarter, Kettle Bridge crossing the Hammer Stream will be found. The origin of the name 'kettle' is not known, but the stream is probably named after the Hammer Mill ironworking site in Biddenden, which this stream passes before reaching Headcorn.

School Stream (a recent name) rises near Pye Corner in Ulcombe and, after meandering through the countryside, passes Hoggs Bridge Green on the southern side. It then passes under Hoggs Bridge on the Ulcombe Road, flows behind the school and under the bridge at the foot of Mill Bank (A274 road) and continues behind Moat Farmhouse to the bridge in Moat Road joining the River Beult just west of the church. It was in this stream that a polished flint axe was found in 1935.

Franks Bridge, Smarden Road, 1920.
Mr Tippen and friend.

The River Sherway joins the River Beult, having passed under Franks Bridge, on the road to Smarden. The bridge was rebuilt in 1917 and nearby is a commemorative stone. Continuing along the Smarden road turn left towards Egerton and take the left fork which brings you to another bridge over the River Sherway. An ancient stone carrying two inscriptions was found here some years ago, but when the bridge was repaired in the autumn of 1984 it was lost. Fortunately, after enquiries, it was re-found, although damaged. It has now been repaired and was resited in November 1986. The inscriptions read as follows:

THIS	THIS
BRIDG BILT	Bridge Rebuilt
IN THE YEARE 1683	in the Year 1846
BY THE CONSTABLES	by Rich'd Fleet & Thos
OF THE HONDRED	Boorman, Constables
OF IRON DANIEL	of the Hundred of Cale
MEDHVRST & ANTHONY DIVE &	Hill & Thos Hodges
YE CONSTABLES OF	Constable of the
YE HONDRED OF CALE	Hundred of Iron.
HILL GEORGE RAIN	
ER & JOHN ABDAY	
O NEWORCKMAN	

Front of Sherway Stone, 1987.   (N. Aldridge)

Stephens Bridge, 1905.

Back of Sherway Stone, 1987.   (N. Aldridge)

THE HIGH STREET AND VILLAGE SHOPS

In 1814 Dearn said: 'Headcorn consists of one wide straggling street of mean houses. The road through it is in no respects superior to the by-ways, being in winter almost impassable for waggons and even in summer too rough for any light carriage. To pass from one side of the street to the other a rough stone causeway is raised to the great annoyance of horsemen at all seasons.' He also calls it 'cheerless and forbidding'. Hasted, at the end of the eighteenth century, called it, 'an unfrequented dull place'.

Mr Arthur Chaplin, a local resident who was born in 1877 at 25 High Street and started work in 1890 in his father's grocery business, recalls that the road was rough, muddy in winter, dusty in spring and summer. The deep ruts made by heavily laden farm wagons made it nearly impassable for light traffic. A narrow footpath of worn flag-stones flanked the north side and after a shower pools of water added discomfort to the pedestrian. A few stepping stones, overgrown with moss, served as a causeway on the opposite side.

Bennett's horse drawn bus outside Maidstone Town Hall on its last journey to Tenterden via Headcorn in 1915. A family concern, Bennett's of Tenterden ran this horse drawn bus service for 130 years. William Burt of Headcorn was employed by R. & J. Bennett as a driver for fifty years.

Many of the present business premises were originally private houses. All shop windows were fitted with small panes of glass which did not lend themselves to display. They also had shutters and, as most of the private houses were similarly equipped, after closing time the street presented a dismal and desolate appearance. Candles and small paraffin lamps were the only means of illumination. Shops were open from 7am-8pm, on Fridays to 9pm and on Saturdays to 10pm. Improvements were gradually made and by the beginning of the First World War most of the businesses would have had new shop fronts with large panes of glass in the windows and shop fittings inside. Earlier closing was instituted in 1890 and Headcorn was one of the first villages to have half-day closing on Wednesdays.

There was no water supply for the village, except a pump near Charity Cottages. As this frequently failed during the dry seasons, many householders in the street had to fetch drinking water from the river, by way of the churchyard and over the level crossing near Beult House. The South Kent Water Co. installed a main's supply between 1888 and 1898. A two-horse bus from Tenterden to Maidstone passed through at 10.20am each day, and carriers' vans also made the journey. It was a tedious business getting to Maidstone, taking over one-and-a-half hours by bus, only varied by walking up Sutton Valence hill. An alternative route by rail via Paddock Wood was an even more trying journey, often entailing a long wait at the junction.

The High Street looking to the Institute from the Colonial Meat Store, No.47, just before 1910.

The interim between the two world wars saw an increase in motor traffic and many visitors from neighbouring villages came to shop in Headcorn, with its wide main street and good selection of shops. Electricity came to the village in 1935, which greatly improved the lighting of premises, but street lighting was not installed until 1959. There was an adequate bus service between Tenterden and Maidstone and occasionally to London provided by the Maidstone and District Bus Company. There were two carriers to Maidstone and local people, by displaying the appropriate card, could arrange for the chosen carrier to call and carry out their requirements.

The mid-1960s brought great changes to the village with the building of housing estates, many of their occupants commuting to London. The village shops were not large enough to cater for the growing demand for their wares and many enlarged their interiors to carry more stock, although the shop fronts retained their original appearance. In 1986 the High Street was completely and most attractively relaid with red concrete brickettes in herringbone design, with the pavements laid in red squares and the parking bays in slate blue. These improvements herald a new era of shopkeepers for many of the familiar names have now gone.

John Evenden standing in the doorway of his shop in 1880. He was a well known saddler and harness maker serving a wide area during the last quarter of the 19th century. The shop, now 21 High Street, has long been used as a newsagent's.

From left to right: George and Ernest Adams, who had a stone mason's shop and yard at North Street in 1920, and George Hooker. The building has retained its original appearance, although it has seen many changes in use from being a bicycle, toy and antiques shop to its present use as a hairdressers.

The High Street looking east, from the George and Dragon, 1908.

Charles James Chaplin standing outside his grocer's and draper's shop, with sons Charles John and Arthur William about 1897. He built this shop and house in 1878 and used his previous shop next door (left of photograph) as a china and hardware store and for storage. The handcart in the photograph had iron tyres and was used to deliver goods. Arthur Chaplin used to push this unwieldy vehicle along the rough roads to Shenley, East End, Stone Stile, Plumtrees, Tong, Fifth Quarter and Chickenden. The shop, at 27 High Street, is still used as a grocer's.

John (Jack) Head outside his saddlery and harness-making shop with Mrs Barham, of Hole Park, Rolvenden, on his right in August 1959. Mr Head came from Staplehurst and was apprenticed by the previous owner, Mr W. Penfold. He took over the business in 1928, this photograph being taken shortly before he retired in 1960. He was a fine craftsman known for miles around. The shop, at 7 Station Road, is now owned by a flooring company.

Mr Q.H. Hyde outside his hardware shop, now 49 High Street, with the second of his five sons, Ernest, in 1927. He was also a builder and lived here until 1928, when he moved to Byways, Oak Lane. The shop is now used as a hairdresser's.

HUBBLE'S HOUSE AND SHOP

This timber-framed house formerly 'Streete House' now 'Tallow House' was probably built in the mid-sixteenth century by a Flemish clothworker. It is believed to have been used as the vicarage by the Rev. Samuel Whiston, who was vicar from 1673-1716. He was one of Headcorn's greatest benefactors and left the ground on the west side of the house for a new vicarage, which was built in 1787. He also left two cottages to the east of the house to the parish, which were demolished in 1959. In the nineteenth century a shop, with a ware-house to the rear, was built adjoining the house on the east side. Mr Arthur Hubble, and his brother Lewis, bought this grocery and drapery shop at the end of the nineteenth century. Mr Arthur Hubble was followed in the business by his son Robert (Bob), who converted the drapery showroom into a Post Office.

Mr Harry Tippen operated the Post Office at the turn of the century at 21 High Street. In 1914 Mrs Philpott took over, first at Home Farmhouse, and then in the mid-1920s moved to 31-33 High Street where Mr Bert Jones succeeded her in 1939. In 1975 Mr Heath was postmaster for two years, succeeded by Mr R. Wood. In 1986 the Post Office was moved to the main area of the shop after the grocery business had been closed and is carried on by Mr David Wood. The original Post Office is now an antique shop selling pine furniture.

Arthur Hubble's eldest daughter, Mrs F. Coveney, ran a private school for boys and girls, up to the age of eleven, in the garden of the house from 1924-1964, known as 'Streete School'.

Mr Charles Brandley and his son Bert inside the bakehouse at No.63 High Street.

Hubble's House and Shop, 1983. There were three grocers and drapers in the High Street, Chaplins, Boormans and Hubble's. The main shop is now the Post Office and on the left is an antique shop.

10

Montpelier House, 59-61 High Street. Built just before the middle of the nineteenth century on the site of a timber-framed house. At the turn of this century A.T. Kemp was the grocer and draper there. He built the row of twelve houses in Oak Lane known as Oakfield Terrace in 1903. Before the First World War, when this photograph was taken, the Tenterden firm of H. Boorman & Co. occupied it and in 1928 it was taken over by their manager, Harry Boorman. In 1963 the property was bought by the National Westminster Bank, who removed the balcony. It is now divided between the bank and an electrical shop.

The High Street looking west about 1868. There is a stone flagged pavement on the right and a post and rail fence around the churchyard. Note also the lack of trees, just the old oak on the left.

This unique picture, although somewhat fuzzy, dates from about 1868 and is the earliest photographic record of the village we have. The old 'George Inn' with is pavement sign can be seen centre right. Beyond is the end wall of 25 High Street, now Hawkes Gunsmiths. The fenced garden is now occupied by 27 High Street, Spar Supermarket.

The old oak in the snow — 1987.
(N. Aldridge)

The Church School, 1910.

HEADCORN SCHOOLS

There was a shortage of school places providing elementary education in Headcorn in 1871, with only the National (Church) School (120 places) and Private Adventure School (20 places) fulfilling the need. As a result the first meeting of the Headcorn School Board was convened on 13th July 1871, in accordance with the terms of the Elementary Education Act of 1870. A census had shown that there was a total of 359 children between the ages of 3 and 13 in the village requiring elementary education. It was agreed that the deficiency in school places be rectified by the provision of a School House and School for 150 children. The site in King's Road was bought for £200 and, after some problems including the bankruptcy of one builder, the school was built for the sum of £1,800. It opened on 5th May 1873 with Joseph Outhwaite as Headmaster, at an initial salary of £100 per annum. In those days school fees were required. The following are early examples:

manual workers 2d. to 6d. (approx. 1p to 2½p) per week
tradesmen and farmers 4d. to 1/- (approx. 1½p to 5p) per week
charges dependent on the grade that the pupil was in.

By the close of the school's first term 83 children had been admitted, though regular attendance by some pupils was poor because they were required to assist in farm work, such as weeding, hop tying and bringing in the harvest. Subjects taught in those early days were handwriting, reading, dictation, arithmetic, singing and, in the upper standards, drawing, needlework, geography and history. Girls generally stayed at school until the age of 12 or 13 years, and boys until 13 to 15 years. From the school records we can see that monetary prizes were awarded for good attendance at the end of each summer term. They varied in 1891 from 1/- (5p) for 350 attendances, to 3/6d. (17½p) for 420 attendances at the higher standards. School fees were abolished in September 1891 as a result of the passing of that year's Education Act and in 1903 the Headcorn Board was replaced by a committee, which became known as the Headcorn Council School.

In December 1901 it ceased to be necessary to draw water from the pump in the school grounds as the South Kent Water Co. connected the main water supply to the school. However, it was not until August 1936 that electric lights were installed, at last dispensing with the old oil lamps. With the arrival of Mr H.E. (Gaffer) Ward in 1905 several innovations and progressive changes were made in the operation and curriculum of the school. These included evening classes for older lads and such subjects as cottage gardening, woodwork and cooking. A school canteen was opened in 1920 to provide dinner for the pupils; the meals were not subsidised, with a charge of 3d. (approx 1½p) per meal being levied.

During the wartime periods the school was active, providing some of its own food from the gardens and also sending socks, shirts and other items for the soldiers and sailors in the 1914-18 war. In December 1914 the children sent to each ex-pupil at the war front a parcel containing useful garments made by them, together with little gifts, such as laces, vaseline, peppermints, cigarettes and chocolates. During the 1939-45 war the school played host to a party of boys from the Downham Central School. Pupils also assisted during the harvest on local farms when required. Thus the school has continued until today, with its growth to nearly 400 pupils in 1973 and the provision of new buildings. However, part of the original building is still used for the Junior School, although part has since been converted into the village library.

Headcorn School taken in 1905 by the Headmaster, Mr H.E. Ward.

Headcorn Council School 1917-27
by G.E. Chantler

The Day of Fear — from which we strive
Began, when at the age of five
From Home quite early I departed,
And serious education started.

When, not accustomed to the noise,
They sat me down among the boys,
I'd had four sisters all my years,
And all these boys — brought me to tears.

My teacher, Mrs Ernie Ward,
A crying boy could not afford,
With smiling face and tears all brimming,
They sat me down among the women.

Having won my confidence,
In time we did big sums in pence,
Dividing, Adding and Subtracting,
The rules to me were most exacting.

As time went on, 'twas quite a while,
To Fanny, I became a Trial,
The Climax came — she settled me,
By caning me behind the knee.

The man that I remember most,
He filled the School Headmaster's Post,
In Handicraft and how to Garden,
Dear Gaffer Ward, I beg your pardon.

I s'pose we really can't expect,
This record here to be correct,
There really is no need to mention,
As kids — we didn't PAY ATTENTION!

A group of Headcorn School staff, with Mr Taylor in the front row c1900.

A group of pupils at Headcorn School c1890, with Mr Taylor, the Headmaster, on the left. Ethel and Sarah Butcher, are back row right and front row second right.

A group of infant pupils at Headcorn School, 1926.

Mr H.E. 'Gaffer' Ward, from the Kentish Express 10th January 1936.

Pupils working in the School gardens in 1924.

A group of pupils at Headcorn School in 1924 with the Headmaster, Mr H.E. Ward, on the right.

The Cloth Hall in 1904 when it was known as 'The Old Workhouse'.

Miss C.M. Elliot (seated), the Headmistress of the Infants School from February 1916 to September 1937, with two other teachers.

Drawing of carved brace on the west wall of an upper room in the Cloth Hall by Violet Outhwaite.

Drawing of Crown posts in the roof of the Cloth Hall by Violet Outhwaite, 1905.

THE CLOTH HALL, NORTH STREET

This impressive structure, built probably in the early sixteenth century, was used in connection with the cloth weaving industry. The wealth generated by this industry was largely responsible for many of the lovely timbered buildings in the parish. The Cloth Hall was used as a collection and distribution centre for the weavers of Headcorn. Here all the cloth woven from local wool was checked for quality, measured for correct width and colour, packed and finally sealed by a local official who regulated this highly organised trade. The cloth would have been stored upstairs awaiting shipment to other parts of the country and abroad. It is quite likely that at the south end of the hall was a hoist to enable bulky objects to be lifted up to the first floor.

The building is a large structure measuring some 60ft long by 18ft wide. Originally there were three halls open to the roof, the main one being to the south in a position well lit by an oriel window, later removed. The spandrels of the braces supporting the roof exhibit some interesting carvings, including a symbolic representation of a chess 'rook'. It has been suggested that the family of Boddenden, or Boddenham, who lived nearby at Biddenden, may have had some connection with the Cloth Hall. Their coat of arms comprised three chess 'rooks' and they were also wealthy cloth merchants.

The building has at various times been used as dwellings, the village workhouse, a bakery and, at present (1987), as offices, estate agents, saddlers and swimming pool contractors.

THE INSTITUTE

The Institute was built by James Chambers and Son, a local builder, in 1866 for the Mutual Improvement Society so that local residents had somewhere to meet other than the local public houses. The ground floor had two rooms, one a library, the other a reading room. Upstairs one large room covered the entire floor and various lectures, music recitals and concerts took place there. The Headcorn Hall Company was formed and many local residents bought shares at two shillings and sixpence each (12½p).

By the turn of the century the library was discontinued and the ground floor turned into a cycle shop. Mr Hildridge was the tenant, but after the First World War Mr Teddy Harden took over. He was a well-liked and familiar character in the High Street, always willing to help cyclists. Upstairs the hall was used by village organisations for flower shows, whist drives, film shows, meetings and the like. The Headcorn Hall Company was dissolved in 1977 and the property sold. Today the ground floor is used as a greengrocer's, the upstairs as a hairdressing salon.

Percy Hawkridge and Tom Longhurst outside the cycle shop at the Institute in the early days of this century.

A group of Methodist chapel members on their outing to Wannock Gardens, Sussex, in 1953.

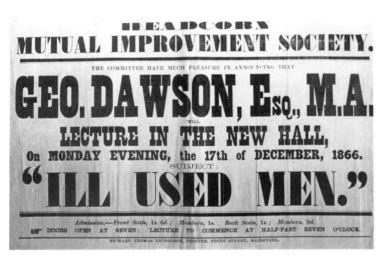

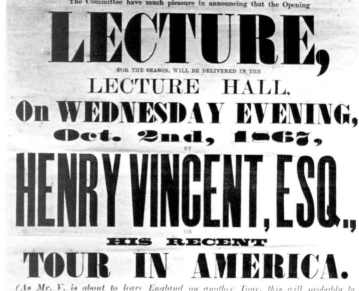

Two nineteenth century posters advertising events in the Institute.

Headcorn Bonfire Night Celebrations, 1950. Headcorn Gardeners' Society First Prize-winning float entitled, 'Pick 'em, Dry 'em, Drink 'em'. Left to right are: N. Hale, S. Watts, S. Peen, S. Harden, and F. Piper.

Headcorn Silver Jubilee Jubilation.
May 6th 1935.

HEADCORN GARDENERS SOCIETY

Headcorn Gardeners' Society

Winners of the First Prize for the "Best Tableau" in the Procession (Local Bodies)
Names (left to right) E. C. Whatman, H. T. Packham, B. Boorman, L. George, P. Fullbrook, J. K. Dane.

Headcorn Gardeners' Society with their winning entry for the Silver
Jubilee Jubilation, held on 6th May 1935.

Back Row: L. CHAPLIN, R. MAYNARD, G. HAYBITTLE, S. HAWKINS, Mr. OUTHWAITE,
T. SHERSBY, J. SKILTON, G. BOORMAN, G. KNIGHT
J. WHITE, J. KNIGHT

Headcorn Cricket Team in 1926, taken at Winchet Hill.

1935 — The Silver Jubilee of King George V and Queen Mary. Mr
George Mercer of Tilden Farm is seen driving his carriage outside the
George and Dragon as part of the village procession held to celebrate
that event. Mr Johnny Paige is the passenger on the right.

THE VILLAGE HALL

Until 1932 all village events needing a hall had either to use 'The Institute' in the High Street, with its flight of steps to the upper floor; go across Parsonage Meadow to the Church School (not so enticing on a bad winter's night); or, for a short time, 'Moat Hall' at the rear of a wheelwright's shed in Moat Road was available, also upstairs. None of the alternatives was particularly attractive so when the Oddfellows decided to build a hall in Station Road it was a very welcome amenity for the village. It was not immediately forthcoming, however, having originally been proposed in 1907 and again in 1911, each time the proposal being turned down.

At last in May 1931 the dream to build the hall became a reality and the project was finally approved. The work commenced in September 1931 and was completed in April the following year. The architect was Mr H.T.B. Barnard and Mr J.H. Gibson the builder. It cost £1,226 to build, but with the purchase of furniture and other fittings the total expenditure was £1,600, which was met by the Loyal Weald of Kent Lodge (No. 6841) of Oddfellows — Headcorn Oddfellows, who had a capital of £10,000 at that time. The hall included a stage, with storage beneath, and a dressing room. It was opened by Lord Cornwallis on Saturday, 28th May 1932 and, after the opening ceremony, entertainment was provided by local residents.

Commencement of building the Oddfellows Hall in 1931 by men from the firm of J.H. Gibson.

This view shows the foundations dug for the Oddfellows Hall in 1931.

Many local organisations used the Oddfellows Hall and it was a great asset to the village. After the Second World War there was a decline in the number of Oddfellows members and when eventually they decided to sell the hall the parish responded with an offer. In June 1964 it was bought for £2,500 with the Parish Council acting as Custodian Trustees. A village hall committee was set up to manage the everyday running of the hall. The name was changed from the 'Oddfellows Hall' to 'The Village Hall' and in 1966 an extension was built to the front, which included an entrance hall with ladies' and gentlemen's cloakrooms. Early in 1971 it was extended on the east side, with the bar and kitchen facilities extended and improved. The hall continues to be the centre of village activities and is still administered by the Village Hall Committee on behalf of the parish council.

A 'Creamery Party' when Mr Coker was manager, held in the Oddfellows Hall, Christmas 1932.

Headcorn Gardeners' Society Dinner 1936, one of the many events held in the Oddfellows Hall.

SHAKESPEARE HOUSE

This house, dating from the sixteenth century, is situated on the south side of the High Street. Shakespeare House (the name has no local significance apart from the period) has a steeply pitched gable end and was probably the main centre of the Headcorn cloth weaving industry in the late sixteenth and seventeenth centuries. Unlike the Cloth Hall, which has a crownpost roof, it utilises side purlins and arch braces. This design was adopted probably because it uses less timber and was therefore cheaper to construct. The house dates from the decade 1580/1590 when this type of roof evolved. The weaving would have been done in a lofty first floor room some 32ft by 17ft. The bulky looms would have needed considerable space and the provision of adequate lighting must have caused a few problems to these rural artisans.

After the cloth trade declined the house saw various changes in use. It overlooked the village green and market place and so was in a good position to become a public house, when it was known as the 'Queen Adelaide'. However, the behaviour of some locals at the annual Leanstock Fair held on 12th June caused the hostelry and the fair to be closed down in the nineteenth century. In the 1950s Shakespeare House was completely restored.

Shakespeare House in 1904.

CHEQUERS

Next to Shakespeare House stands Chequers, so named from the time when it was a hostelry called 'The Ball and Chequers'. It is basically a hall house of about 1480, with a cross wing added later to the western end. The building has previously been divided into three cottages, one of which was used as a tea shop in the 1920s.

Chequers and Shakespeare House, 1954.

Chequers and Shakespeare House, 1919.

Rear view of the Barn in Wheeler Street, during reconstruction in 1984. (N. Aldridge)

Grigg Farmhouse, from the west, in 1906. The house has the date 1718 on the front, but it is probably older. The large pond in front was reputed to be dug out for marl in 1710.

The Gate House with turnpike gates before 1880. The tollgate has not operated on the Smarden and Biddenden roads leading out of the village since 1880, but the cottage today still looks much as it did in the last century.

Chantry Farm Stables, Grigg Lane, 1987.
(N. Aldridge)

CHANTRY FARM AND KENTISH MANURE WORKS

This lovely old farmhouse, set back on the corner of Oak Lane and Grigg Lane, is probably several hundred years old. It was one of the four manors of Headcorn. In 1466 the land on which the farmhouse stands was given to support a chantry chapel founded in the parish church by Thomas and Robert Kent. The stables adjoining Grigg Lane, with their undulating roofs of Kentish peg tiles, present a charming rural scene.

Next to Chantry Farm, on the corner of Grigg Lane and Oak Lane, stands the building that housed the Kentish Manure Works. Artificial manure was brought by train to Headcorn and mixed for distribution to local farmers. The business operated from the 1890s to about the time of the First World War.

QUEEN ELIZABETH I

In the summer of 1573 'Good Queen Bess' made a Royal Progress through Kent, leaving Greenwich Palace on 14th July and not returning until ten weeks later. She stayed overnight in some of the richest houses in the south-east of England, such as Knole, Hemsted (now Benenden Girls School), Sissinghurst Castle and Westenhanger. The owners of these properties were expected not only to pay for the queen's enormous retinue, but also to present valuable gifts to her upon her departure.

In mid-August Elizabeth visited Cranbrook and stayed for four days at Sissinghurst Castle, where she received two silver cups. She then travelled on to Smarden where the royal grant to hold a weekly market, which had originally been conferred by Edward II, was renewed. There is a record in the Smarden Churchwardens' accounts as follows: 'item 6d. paid to ye ryngers when the Queenes Majestye was here'.

Elizabeth spent three days at the manor house at Boughton Malherbe, four miles north-east of Headcorn, and almost certainly passed through the village on her way there. There is a local tradition that she rested in one of the houses connected with the cloth industry in the High Street. Legend also says that she admired the fields of ripening corn in the area and decreed that henceforth 'Hedecrone' should be known as Headcorn, owing to the large heads of corn there.

Home Farm, High Street. Although this house appears to be built of brick, it is faced with mathematical tiles, the only complete example in Headcorn. (N. Aldridge)

Rushford Manor taken in 1905 when the main sewer was being laid in the High Street.

RUSHFORD MANOR, BARN AND COTTAGES

Rushford Manor was the original manor of Headcorn. In the reign of Edward II it was held by Adam de Rishford. The Lord of the Manor exercised manorial rights over the roadside verges and common land and any stray animals were liable to be impounded until the owners had paid the necessary dues. The present house dates from the seventeenth century.

On the other side of the road stands Manor Cottage, which was built as a barn, and later converted to cottages. Next door stands another house also called Manor Cottage, with an unusually high brick chimney stack. This is probably explained by the fact that the original roof was damaged by fire and the replacement was erected at a lower pitch. Originally several cottages, it has now been converted to one house, and completes this group of manor associated dwellings.

The barn, Wheeler Street. The interior showing the front door of original hall house, taken during restoration in 1984.   (N. Aldridge)

WHEELER STREET HALL HOUSE - AROUND 1400 AD
A   RECONSTRUCTION.

N.R.A.
1984.

Drawing of The Barn in Wheeler Street as it would have appeared in 1400 when it was a hall-house. Reputed to be the oldest domestic dwelling in Headcorn, it is now divided into two houses. (N. Aldridge)

The house on the right was a barn before its conversion into three cottages. In the centre of the view, the two cottages obscured by trees were part of the Rushford Manor complex. Photograph dated 1907.

A haymaking scene in 1916, showing the Butcher and Wood families of Headcorn and Smarden.

GEOLOGY AND AGRICULTURE

Headcorn lies on an outcrop of Weald Clay some 5 miles wide, traversed by the River Beult. Small ridges occur around the village some of which, such as Mill Bank, consist of a harder rock known as Paludina Limestone, or Bethersden Marble. The name is taken from a fresh-water snail whose fossilised shells are closely packed together in the rock. They give the rock a distinctly knobbly appearance when it is used as a building stone. Examples of its use can be seen in Headcorn church, the stone probably being dug at Kelsham. Although sometimes known as Bethersden Marble, it is not a true marble, but is capable of taking a high shine and so has been used extensively for interior decoration. Until the middle of the last century the Weald was notorious for its bad roads. In wet weather they were knee-deep in mud; in dry spells of spring and early summer the ruts of iron-hard clay caused similar hardships for travellers. As a means of overcoming this problem footpaths made of slabs of Bethersden Marble were laid and became a common feature of this countryside. Such a path still exists on both sides of Pell Bridge. The shallow quarries where the stone was extracted can still be seen at Kelsham and Hazelpits.

There are many other pits in the area which were originally dug for marl and have since filled with water to form small ponds. Marling was a process of fertilising the land with ground rock, consisting of clay minerals, calcite, aragonite and silt. It was a common practice throughout the Middle Ages right up to this century, where it has been replaced by modern chemical fertilisers. There are records from the Assize Courts of Henry III's reign of numerous accidents, some fatal, to workers employed in the marl pits.

Farming techniques have changed greatly since the first 'dens' were opened as clearings in the old wealden forests and used as sites for grazing. The woodland was gradually cut down and the heavy Weald Clay used for sheep grazing and milk production. It was found that the climate and properties of the clay were also good for fruit and hop growing, thus the area around Headcorn developed a wealth of mixed farms. Modern day agricultural policies seem to be changing all this, however, together with more powerful farming equipment and better drainage. The fields are becoming larger and arable is replacing the mixed farming of former times. Sadly, there is now only one farm in the village still growing hops, a considerable change when one considers that only a few years ago almost every farm had a hop garden, as can be seen by the number of oasthouses that still dot the landscape. Competition with better growing areas and with Europe has also ensured a decline in fruit growing.

Loading sheaves of corn for Mr Alfred Day of Tong Farm, in 1943. On the left are Mr Charlie Sharp and on the top of the wagon is Miss Nancy Sharp.

A hog fatted by Mr Henry Kingsnorth of Kelsham Farm, April 1815. It weighed 76 stone 7 lb!

HOP PICKING

During September of each year thousands of Londoners flocked to Kent for the hop picking season. Many arrived on special trains at Headcorn station where they were ferried by cart to local farms. There they would stay in rudimentary accommodation, known locally as hopper huts, often with only straw for beds. However, for many this was their summer holiday as they came from the crowded East End of London and it was the only chance their children had of seeing the countryside.

For Headcorn this invasion brought problems as well as prosperity. Many shops closed their doors and removed their front windows to serve people. Additional police were drafted into the village to assist

Mr Bingham of Home Farmhouse in 1924. He was hop booker at Tong Farm for several years.

Local hop pickers at Oak Farm in 1938. From left to right are Sarah Butcher, Mrs Ethel Aldridge, Beaty Martin and Mr Fred Aldridge.

Mr Alfred Day's workmen at Tong Farm with a full hop pocket in September 1938.

the hard pressed local bobby. At weekends special trains brought the husbands of the families — cost of the return journey was 1/6d. (7½p) as can be seen on a ticket from London Bridge to Headcorn in the York National Railway Museum. They joined their wives in spending some of the week's wages celebrating in the local public houses, from where songs of the East End of London could be heard in the High Street.

All this activity ended with the coming of automated hop picking machines. With only a few workers being required, most of these were obtained from the local community. Sadly, no more are the sounds of 'get your hops ready' and 'measure' heard in the hop gardens of Kent.

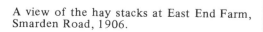

A view of the hay stacks at East End Farm, Smarden Road, 1906.

HEADCORN MILLS

It is believed that at one time there were four windmills in the Parish of Headcorn. The two windmills known within living memory stood on the Millbank and were known as Black Mill and White Mill. They were both eight-sided smock mills of four floors.

There is perhaps no better way to relate the history of these mills than to quote the words of Thomas Witherden Burden and his grandson, Sydney Burden:

'The advent of windmills into this country was of early date and by old writers stated to have been introduced by the early crusaders who found them in use by the Saracens. Chaucer and later Shakespeare both allude to them — who that has read Chaucer's "Canterbury Tales" doesn't remember the miller and his attire — "a white coat and a blue hood wore he . . . " and how "on bagpipes he did play".

'Headcorn, from its flat surface in the valley of the Beult, did not lend itself to water power so that of necessity windpower became the vogue. On Motynden Farm, site of a priory, is a field called "Farthing Green" with a low mound always formerly known as "The Millfield", probably dating from the days of the friars and having a post windmill for the purpose of grinding corn. Tradition also says that some 150 years since there existed a post windmill at Tattlebury which belonged to the family of Swaffer. On surveying the spot this appears very probable — a road leads to an old cottage and garden still in use beyond which, in the small enclosure now united with other fields, stood the ancient mill worked for many years by the family. In the list of charitable donations there appears from the will of Thomas Swaffer dated 1648 a gift of 15/- per annum to the poor of Headcorn from the house and land at Tattlebury.

White Mill floodlit for the coronation of King George VI in 1937.

'On the bases of these old picturesque post mills there arose those with which we are more familiar — the two large bodied smock mills on the millbank just above the village. The oldest of these, which was pulled down in 1910, was for many years known as the Black Mill from its having been tarred instead of painted during the last 50 years of its existence. It was a large picturesque erection and for many years did a quantity of work for the district. It was built in 1786 by a William Boorman who, to distinguish him from another of the same name, was called from his trade "Timberbroker Boorman". It was used early in the last century by the Ottaways and afterwards for many years by George Mercer Senior, who resided nearby. He built the ugly but useful steam mill near the windmill which was removed by the present owner when the windmill was taken away. For the last 50 years of its life it was used by Thomas Burden Senior, who founded the Seed Store in the village, and subsequently by his son, Thomas Witherden Burden. The sweeps were removed about 1900 and it was used as a store until its demolition about 1910. The first house on the left going up Blackmill Hill is exactly on the site and incorporates some 18,000 re-used bricks from the windmill and steam mill.

Black Mill, built in 1786 and demolished in 1910, showing the chimney of the steam mill built in 1846.

The White Mill looking towards the south east in 1929.

White Mill and the Mill Cottage, 1914.

The White Mill before demolition in 1952.　　(Kent Messenger)

Mill Bank, Headcorn, 1910.

'The only mill then remaining was the White Mill — so called from its being painted that colour all its life. This was built about 1814 by Ralph, the Sissinghurst millwright, for William Boorman who was second cousin of the one who built the Black Mill and which for over 100 years had only four tenants — two Burdens, and two Boormans, two very old family names in the village.

'Thomas Witherden Burden gave up the White Mill in 1916 when East Sutton Estate was sold. Bidding only went to £330 and the mill was withdrawn. Subsequently it was sold, together with brick and slate stabling (now added to and in private use) and over 3 acres of land for £350 to Alf Millen of Maplehurst, who owned the water mill at Frittenden. It then passed to his son and was last used shortly before the Coronation of King George VI in 1937. It was floodlit for the Coronation and although not in good repair was still in working order. Mr Millen junior sold it about that time and it passed to another who spent virtually nothing on repairs or weather proofing. She was never again repainted. Thomas Witherden Burden last painted her in 1914. During World War Two one of the middlings broke and she shed one of her sweeps.

'The White Mill again changed hands and the stable and wagon shed were converted into a small house and the owner could only afford to keep the mill standing by heavily shoring up the inside with huge oak beams. On the death of that owner the mill and house were bought by Maurice Fermor, the builder of Chartaway Street, East Sutton. He offered it to the Parish Council for the village and to the Kent County Council, who discussed for a very long time whether or not to buy it. In the end Mr Fermor pulled it over with a tractor. The house known as Whitemill incorporates the wagon house and stable, but is now much bigger. We were very sad to see the end of the White Mill — it was a tragedy for the village.'

The mill was pulled down in 1952 as it would have cost over £4,000 to restore.

The White Mill demolished in 1952.
(Kent Messenger)

The Forge with Mr George Bowles, centre, and his son James, aged nine, second on the left, in 1871.

THE FORGES

At the beginning of this century there were four forges in the Parish of Headcorn, but by the middle of the century there were none. The forge at Hawkenbury ceased very early in this century and became a private house. The forge in Lenham Road, at the junction with the lane to Southernden, lasted a little longer, but is now a farm store. A member of the Bowles family was blacksmith there.

The forge in Forge Lane, which had two furnaces, continued to operate until 1932 when the blacksmith, George Laker, died. He had taken over from George Prebble at the end of the last century. He lived in Forge House, alongside the forge, with his wife and five daughters. In addition to making horseshoes and shoeing horses, Mr Laker repaired farm implements and made and fixed iron tyres on farm waggons and carts. He also repaired household articles such as fire irons, trivets and hinges and was especially interested in creating decorative wrought iron work. When he died the anvil sounded no more, but a fitting tribute to a village craftsman can be seen in the churchyard, where there is a memorial to him in the form of a stone anvil with adze, chisel, hammer, tongs, punches and a horseshoe. One of his daughters, Mary Laker, has written about her childhood at the forge in her book, 'Vulcan's Daughters', which is available locally. The old forge is now used as a garage.

There was also a forge some 200-300 years old standing close to the junction of Ulcombe Road and Lenham Road, but the increase in traffic in recent years caused it to be demolished to provide better visibility. The earliest records of this forge date from the late eighteenth century when two brothers, James and Thomas Kingsnorth, were the blacksmiths. They sold 'The Olde Forge' land and two houses on 7th October 1823 for £450. Edward King took over the tenancy. On 12th October 1866 George Bowles bought the contents of the Forge from Frederick Wakefield for £48.15s.0d. He lived in Forge House and had four sons, all of whom were apprenticed as blacksmiths and

had forges of their own in nearby villages. It was his youngest son James who succeeded him at 'The Olde Forge', in King's Road.

It was a typical country forge with two hearths and anvils, a water trough with tools hanging along the side and a bench strewn with tools and other oddments. Spanning the centre of the forge was an enormous oak beam, probably a ship's timber as evidenced by the mortice cuts. The treviss was added in the early nineteenth century. It was partitioned off from the forge and was the only part to see change as doors were added towards the end of the century. The forge door was in two parts and covered with initials burnt in by Mr Bowles when he tried out his handiwork, before marking the farm or garden tools of local people.

Mr Bowles began his apprenticeship when he was 14 years old, receiving 6d. a week the first year, 1/6d. the second, 2/- the third and then an increase of 1/- a year until it was completed. He worked from 6am to 7pm with breaks at 8am for breakfast and 1pm for dinner. He could remember a team of oxen pulling up at the forge to be shod while travelling between fairs. When he was young the horseshoe nails were made by hand and he used to go out in frosty weather at 3am to the various stables to fix frost nails. He also repaired farm implements and made wrought iron gate brackets, hinges and other ornate work. There was a wheelwright's shop on the site of King's Road Stores during last century and he worked in conjunction with the owner putting metal tyres on farm cart wheels and other work. Later he worked in conjunction with Mr W. Cashford, builder and wheelwright, in King's Road. He was joined in later years by his son-in-law, Mr Courtney Bridger. Mr Bridger retired after the Second World War and was succeeded by Mr E.W. Jeffery, but when he died in 1946 the forge was never used again.

Two brothers named Percy later acquired it and sold tools and hardware, along with a little welding, until it was demolished in 1965.

The Forge at the corner of Ulcombe Road and Lenham Road in 1920. James Bowles is second on the left and Courtney Bridger second right.

James Bowles and Courtney Bridger, with his daughter Betty, in 1929.

Mr Harry Tippen's Ariel 9 motor car in the High Street in 1927. Driving it is Frank Tippen, Harry's son. Binnie, his wife, and one of their sons is sitting in the front seat with Nellie Tippen and their other son in the back.

HEADCORN FIRE BRIGADE

The Headcorn Fire Brigade came into being at a meeting in the Kings Arms Inn on Tuesday 9th April 1907, where Mr W.H. Ruff proposed the forming of the Headcorn Fire Brigade Committee. Initially there were 10 members, which soon increased to 15 (about the same number as today) under the captaincy of Mr C.P. Kingsland. He remained as captain until 1928.

To fight fires the village arranged for a number of fire hydrants to be provided at various points around the village area — free if used to fight a fire, but a small charge was imposed if used for practice. The fire fighting appliance was a hand cart with hoses, connectors, standpipe and hydrant key. It was kept in a store at 'The Chequers', in the High Street: twenty years later it was moved to 'Oakdene', Forge Lane, and later still to a temporary room at the 'Kings Arm's'. It was not until 1937 that the Parish Council built the first small wooden fire station in the Manor Farm yard, next to Rushford Manor, the site loaned by Mr Jesse Tassell.

The members of the now officially titled 'Headcorn Fire Brigade' were summoned by firing a maroon from a mortar purchased from Messrs Brock and Co. at a cost of £1.11s.3d. Payment for attendance at a fire was at a rate of 2/- per hour for the first hour and 6d. for the second and subsequent hours. Owners of property were required to pay for services rendered, an incentive to be careful. This system remained in operation until 1938.

The first fire attended was on 16th January 1910 at North Street, for which the committee was paid 12/-. Fire fighting was restricted to the village area, where there were hydrants. Personal equipment such as helmets and boots were not available in those days and only appeared from 1925 onwards, when they were purchased by the Parish Council. For some time after Mr Kingsland's resignation in 1928 interest in the brigade declined. It was not until 1936, at the instigation of Mr Alfred Day, Chairman of the Parish Council, that the brigade was reorganised and properly equipped. Mr Day presented the service with a Dennis No. 1 trailer pump, which was towed by a converted car given by John Charles and Frank Foreman in memory of their fathers. Uniforms, helmets, axes and the like were acquired over the next few years. The captain at that time was Frank Tassell.

After the outbreak of war in 1939, the brigade left Parish ownership, coming under the control of Hollingbourn Rural District Council until it became part of the National Fire Service. New appliances were provided at this time. The final change in administration came in 1948 when Kent County Council took control. Since then the Fire Station has moved from its Manor Farm site to the existing site next to the railway station. Two fire stations have since been erected. The first opened in May 1953 and was of fairly austere construction due to the difficulty in obtaining traditional materials. The latest was built on the same site and was opened in 1978 by Sir John Wells. Also to be seen at the rear of this station is another building which housed the Auxiliary Fire Service 'Green Goddess' machine until the unit's disbandment in the 1970s.

Aftermath of the fire at the bakery in the Cloth Hall, North Street, 1927.

The original scout hut destroyed by fire in 1945.

Fire in the bakery at Cloth Hall, North Street, 5th November 1927.

Headcorn Fire Brigade in 1937, taken after a fire at Chequers in the High Street. From left to right are: F. Tassell, J. Ford, N. Ovenden, L. Sylvester, E. Bye, A. Chapman, S. Burden and F. Marshall.

Demonstration of a new pumping appliance in the school playground by the Fire Brigade in 1935.

Mediaeval barn destroyed by fire on 19th September 1966 at Moat Farm.

Headcorn Station in 1890. The Station Master is on the right wearing a top hat.

HEADCORN STATION

In 1842 the South Eastern Railway came to Headcorn when the Redhill to Ashford Line was opened. This took place in stages: Redhill—Tonbridge on 26th May, Tonbridge—Headcorn 31st August and Headcorn—Ashford on 1st December. The present station building dates from that time, the exterior having changed very little. The layout was changed from an arrangement of staggered platforms to the present one of platforms opposite each other. This work was started in 1924 when the line was quadrupled, a new footbridge and signal box erected and platforms for S.R. and Kent and East Sussex Railway trains installed. The whole operation was completed in 1930.

In 1905 the K. & E.S.R. opened its branch line from Tenterden to Headcorn and remained independent until 1948, when it became part of British Railways. With the opening of this line it became possible to travel to London via Headcorn or Robertsbridge. It played quite an important part in both world wars, carrying equipment and, in the 1939-1945 conflict, food to depots at Tenterden.

The line was reasonably successful, but by 1932 had become unprofitable. Prior to 1954, when the line was closed, a sample survey taken during one week showed that only 118 passengers travelled on 90 trains, some trains running empty. The track was lifted in 1955 and standing now on the footbridge looking to the 'up' platform, it is difficult to realise that a railway once existed on this scrub-covered wasteland.

During the Dunkirk episode of the Second World War the station was the scene of great activity. Here was the first stop from the Channel ports and a unit of the R.A.S.C., plus many local people, fed the British, French, Belgian, Dutch and Polish servicemen. About 100 trains a day, for 12 days, called here and made a halt for eight minutes. It was reported that one bakery produced 50,000lbs of bread daily and often about 5,000 eggs were cooked. Beef was also cooked on spits by the line to provide mountains of sandwiches. Other food halts were made at Paddock Wood and Faversham.

This was perhaps the greatest single episode involving Headcorn and its people, but at an earlier date, in 1865, an accident which occurred to the west of Headcorn must have caused quite a stir. During repairs to the line a section of track was removed. A boat train from Dover, which ran irregularly according to the tides, arrived unexpectedly and was derailed. Among the passengers returning from the Continent was Charles Dickens, who helped with the injured. At a later date another famous passenger was King Edward VII, who often alighted here when en route to East Sutton, continuing his journey by carriage.

Headcorn Station in 1987.   (A. Howe)

31

Layout of Headcorn Station in May 1955, looking east. (L.J. Daniels)

Headcorn Station, May 1955, taken from the Kent and East Sussex railway line. (L.J. Daniels)

Looking east from the footbridge at Headcorn Station in 1938, showing the main line and the Kent and East Sussex branch line. (S.W. Baker)

A similar view today, looking east from the footbridge at Headcorn Station in 1987.
(A. Howe)

Headcorn Station in 1916, showing troops in the goods yard.

Station Road in 1910. The house on the left was the home of Harry Gibson, builder, until he moved to Wheeler Street in about 1920. The two shops alongside were owned by F. Murrell, butcher, and Mr Jeffery, hairdresser, which later became Verrall's, the Chemist, until they were demolished about 1923. Mr S. Burbridge built a garage on the site which is still there today. His father, James Burbridge, used to hire out horse drawn carriages and lived in the house next-door. On the right of the picture is the Railway Hotel, built soon after the railway came to Headcorn in 1842. It was demolished in 1982 and is now the site of Knowles Gardens retirement homes.

Uplands, Mill Bank, taken in 1916 when it was used as the Headcorn Auxiliary Military Hospital. The photograph shows a group of patients with Mr Charles Foreman (in straw hat), with his wife, Maud, on his right. His daughters Dorothy and Enid are in front and beside him, respectively. His son Jack is seated on the ground on the right of the picture and son Charles is on the ground at the extreme left.

WORLD WAR I — 1914-1918

At the outbreak of World War I Headcorn was a pleasant village with a population of 1,300, mainly dependent on agriculture for a living. The only military target was the main line railway which ran from London to Dover, passing through the parish from west to east, just south of the High Street. Although nothing like the activities of World War II took place here in World War I and Headcorn saw no enemy action, there was quite a lot of activity in the village.

Troops were stationed here, mostly of the Sussex Reservists. A cookhouse and wooden barracks were erected on a small field (now built over) in Wheeler Street to accommodate them. While this was being built they were billeted with families in the village. They numbered between fifty and one hundred at any one time. One of the original buildings was still there in World War II and was used for storage. The troops were responsible for guarding the railway line and roads, especially at night.

The 'Fencibles', similar to World War II Home Guard units, was formed with H.E. Ward Esq. (Headmaster of the local school) in charge. It consisted of men and boys not already in the services or on essential war work. The special constabulary was also on duty to keep watch on Biddenden and Frittenden arches and the station foot-bridge, reporting by the nearest telephone to London any unusual aircraft or lights in the sky. They were the forerunners of the Royal Observer Corps in World War II.

A few light aircraft came over Headcorn and some made forced landings. On one occasion Winston Churchill was a passenger when his plane landed south of the railway line and, while awaiting repairs, he visited the 'Fencibles' who were meeting in the school grounds with Lt. H.E. Ward. A Handley Page bomber with engine trouble came down on the Marl Banks south of the village and had to be cut in sections and taken by lorries to Farnborough. Airships, mainly Zeppelins, which usually approached London via the Thames estuary, sometimes returned following the railway line on moonlit nights. Although some were shot down by gunfire, none fell in this parish.

Many young men from the village were drafted into the services, thirty-seven of whom, sadly, did not return. Women successfully carried on their usual occupations and a great deal of work went into helping the war effort. Headcorn Auxiliary Military Hospital was opened at 'Uplands', Mill Bank, (now Uplands Residential Home), for convalescent overseas soldiers. The first patients were received in December 1914 and when the hospital closed in April 1919, 815 cases had received attention. Mrs Maud Foreman was commandant and Dr R.H. Hardwick was medical officer, while the staff were members of the Red Cross. A committee which ran the hospital on voluntary contributions was able to hand a surplus of £150 to the West Kent General Hospital, Maidstone, when the auxiliary hospital closed.

The light aircraft which crashed at Summer Hill, 26th March 1915.

Troops being fed at Headcorn Station after Dunkirk, 1940.

(Kent Messenger)

THE SECOND WORLD WAR

In between the two world wars, the change in village life was very gradual. The population had increased from 1,300 to 1,450, six houses had been built by Hollingbourn Council on the western side of Mill Bank, another three further along on the opposite side of the road and four more in Wheeler Street. Private houses had also been built, mainly in Maidstone Road, and bungalows in Grigg Lane, with others more sporadic. Small mixed farms continued to be the main source of employment, although in 1921 a small dairy was built close to the river, now the site of Unigate, in Biddenden Road. It prospered and by 1939 was owned by 'South Eastern Farmers' employing several Headcorn men.

Traffic increased, especially in the 1930s with the advent of the popular motor car, and on Sundays in summer they streamed through the village en route to the coast. Several London cycling clubs used the straight road for trials on Sundays. The main road remained unaltered, but some of the minor roads were considerably improved. Village life still centred very much around the church, the chapels and school. Existing societies flourished, including the Gardeners, Oddfellows, Cricket, Football and Tennis Clubs, and new ones were formed, such as the British Legion for men and women, the Women's Institute, Boy Scouts, Girl Guides, Toc H, the Dramatic Society and an orchestra.

In 1938 the school was used for lecture courses for the Special Police, Air Raid Wardens and Observer Corps, as well as for public meetings to advise residents what to expect if war was declared. Earlier, in 1937, Mr Charles Kingsland had been approached and had accepted the post of Head Warden. He was solely responsible for Headcorn under the Hollingbourn Rural District Council, who were the local authority responsible for air raid precautions. He recalls that the response for volunteers was more than adequate to maintain the essential services. Identity cards, gas masks, and Anderson and Morrison Shelters were all distributed to the local inhabitants. On 28th August 1939 the local school teachers stood-by to receive children evacuated from London at the station and send them by

coaches to the surrounding villages. Headcorn itself had the pupils from Downham Central School, who were billeted in the village and attended the local school, assisted by their staff. Some remained for the duration of the war, including one master and his family, others returning for various reasons.

Headcorn settled into the war years with young men and women called into the armed forces, the emergency services on alert and blackouts enforced, but there was little activity in the opening months. May 1940 saw the evacuation from Dunkirk and Headcorn really rose to the occasion. The whole village helped the Royal Army Service Corps feed the troops as each train load halted at the station for eight minutes. Thousands of sandwiches were cut in the barn at Rushford Manor by the local residents by night and day for twelve days. At the station the Royal Army Service Corps made tea and cooked beef and eggs and every soldier on the trains had food, tea and cigarettes. Altogether 300,000 men were evacuated from Dunkirk, along with 50,000 foreign troops. It was a mammoth task undertaken by untrained local people and a very great credit to the people of Headcorn.

This event was followed that autumn by the blitz on London, with Headcorn situated in what became known as 'Blitz Alley'. Anti-aircraft sites were quickly set up by the army, together with search lights, one being close to the village on the corner of Lenham Road and Forge Lane. Others were sited in the countryside, where troops were stationed and Kelsham farmhouse was requisitioned. The first high explosive bomb fell between Southernden and Sherway on 27th August 1940 at 11.20pm, but caused no damage. On 12th October 1940 seven high explosive bombs fell in a line from Bletchenden to Little Grigg. One of these fell on the south-west corner of Chantry House killing Mrs Jessica Foreman, Miss Mary Foreman, Miss Beatrice Munn and Mr Walter Tassell. Three people on the other side of Grigg Lane were injured. Mr Charles Kingsland recalls many other incidents but no further loss of life. There were a few incidents in the village in 1941, but none in 1942.

In early 1943 the Air Ministry requisitioned land for twelve temporary airfields in Kent. One of these was at Headcorn, one mile south of the village between the River Beult and the lane to Smarden through Shenley Farm. It had two runways aligned east-to-west and north-to-south, the latter crossing the road between White House and Ebenezer Farm. The site was chosen because it was flat, mostly arable or pasture with no trees or ditches allowing quick and easy preparation. It was known as Lashenden Airfield. Conditions were very basic. Shenley House was requisitioned and Nissen Huts and tents were erected. In June 1943 the airfield was ready to receive a reorganised fighter command who were given an intensive training programme until the autumn, when the weather made conditions for aircraft unsuitable. A small maintenance staff remained there during the winter months, some being billeted at Perrin Wood House, Water Lane, which had also been requisitioned.

In the spring of 1944 the Americans came to Headcorn and 354 group of 100 Fighter Wing flying P51 mustangs had their headquarters at Lashenden. In April 353, 355 and 356 Squadrons arrived and were ready for operations in May. They were entertained by the local residents and it was reminiscent of the hop picking days when their London friends descended on the village. On 23rd June 1944 they left for Criqueville, France, having made quite an impact on the village. Before D-Day they had visits from General Eisenhower, General Patton and Marshal of the R.A.F. Lord Trenchard.

On 29th May 1944, at 10.28am an auxiliary petrol tank fell from an American aircraft behind Nos. 45 and 47 in the High Street. Mr Jock Ford, who had a greengrocery business at No. 47 was severely injured and he, Miss Sylvia Ford and Miss Rene Fairway all needed hospital treatment. Four other people were also injured. The house and shop were made uninhabitable and two outbuildings demolished and a motor van destroyed. Mr Percy Daw, who had the newsagents and confectioners at No. 45, was among the injured and his property was also damaged. The American Forces at Lashenden Airfield rushed to assist using foam to control the fire — quite an experience for Headcorn people who had never seen buildings covered in bubbles before! Their medical officer came to assist Dr Robert Hardwick, who was casualty officer that day.

On 15th June 1944, at 11.32pm, the first flying bomb, or doodle-bug, was observed over Headcorn. Again the American Forces at Lashenden Airfield went into action. Local residents who did not know what was happening were very concerned, afterwards describing it as a mammoth firework display. They rushed an anti-aircraft gun to the High Street on the corner with Forge Lane and, together with other anti-aircraft guns sited nearby, much damage was done to roofs and windows. This onslaught continued without a break until around 11.15am the next day. After this, most days saw doodlebugs flying over the village, but only twelve came down in the parish. On 8th July 1944, at 11.22pm, a flying bomb fell opposite Shenley Cottages. Although one cottage contained fourteen people, there were only three minor casualties. Another cottage used as an office and unoccupied at the time was completely wrecked. Another flying bomb fell behind Noah's Ark Cottage, in a meadow at the foot of Summer Hill on 25th August at 07.15am. Mrs Kingsnorth, an elderly widow, was the only occupant and escaped without injury, but the cottage was damaged beyond repair. After the flying bombs came an onslaught of rockets, which all fortunately passed over, none falling in the parish. When the war ended the total number of alerts received was 1,261.

Group photograph of members of the Royal Observer Corps at Headcorn in 1942. Back row: E. Ward, G. Tyrell, H. Packham, H. Shaw, R. Farrance, H. Vidler, R. Sweetman and G. Daniels. Front row: R. Slingsby, A. Hale, R. Collins, S. Burbridge (Head), C. Bridger, P. Daw and W. Field.

Visit of King Peter of Yugoslavia, seen on left, to Lashenden Airfield in May 1944.

Visit of General 'Blood and Guts' Patton to Lashenden Airfield in 1944. General Weyland and Lt. Col. Bickell can also be seen.

The missiles which fell in the parish were

Flying Bombs	12
High Explosive Bombs	33
Unexploded High Explosive Bombs	8
Oil Bombs	3
Fire Bombs, single	4
Containers	2
Total	62

Two dwellinghouses were completely destroyed, along with one group of farm buildings, and 329 buildings received varying degrees of damage. According to the wardens census in 1939 there were 511 houses in the parish.

After the war it was disclosed that secret information had been received in 1941 declaring Headcorn to be an important point in the event of invasion. A special triumvirate was set up with the military Commander in Supreme Control. The vicar, the Rev. Max Bryant, was appointed Civil Head of the parish with Mr Bert Weaver as the police constable. They were to be responsible for the military and civil affairs within the perimeter of the village proper, which was to be cordoned off from the rest of the parish with barbed wire, road blocks, machine gun posts and various other devices. Arrangements were made for food dumps within and outside the perimeter, emergency coal supplies and alternative means of supplying water, lighting and heating were prepared. Exercises were held with the Home Guard, Civil Defence, police and National Fire Service. The rest of the parish was to remain under the control of the Head Warden, Mr Charles Kingsland, and Hollingbourn R.D.C. In the event of the Rev. Max Bryant becoming a casualty, Mr Kingsland would replace him and another Head Warden would be appointed. Fortunately these invasion precautions were never put to the test.

Lt. Col. G. Bickell and USAF friend, at Lashenden Airfield in 1944.

On 5th August 1946 a 'Welcome Home Dinner' was given to servicemen and women returning from the war, together with the land army, and their respective wives and husbands in a large marquee on the cricket field in Lenham Road. About 200 guests sat down to a remarkable meal (considering food rationing was still in force) of cold chicken, potatoes, salad, fruit salad and ice cream. Beer, minerals and cider were also prepared and served by local ladies. Expressions of appreciation were made by the parish council and each local-born guest received a present — a wallet and cigarette case for the men and powder compact for the ladies. It concluded with a cabaret by Marco, of Folkestone.

491st Battery of 21st AAA Group. Ack-ack Gunners, Headcorn 4th July 1944.

Group of Mustang aircraft lined up for the visit of King Peter of Yugoslavia in May 1944, at Lashenden Airfield.

Headcorn residents preparing food for the troops in the barn at Rushford Manor after Dunkirk, 1940.   (Kent Messenger)

The Royal Observer Corps. The first observation post was in Station Meadow, now Rushford Close, photographed in January 1940. Mr E. Ward of Vine Farm is on the left with Mr R. Farrance of 'Brooklands', Kings Road. Shortly after a permanent post was erected in Lenham Road, in the corner of a field near Fifth Quarter Cottages. It was manned continuously for the remainder of the war.

An example of Sommerfield steel planking used for runways and taxiways at Lashenden Airfield during the Second World War. After the war it was used for farm gates, fences and the like.

(N.R. Aldridge)

A uniformed family in 1940. Third from the right is Mr George Jeffery with his son, Ewart, on his right. Both are wearing Home Guard uniforms. Jack Cooper (son-in-law) is on the left wearing a Royal Engineer's uniform and on the right is another son-in-law. Leonard Hawkes, in R.A.F. uniform.

Mrs Margaret Cooper on the left with her sister, Kate Jeffery, in their wartime Anderson shelter in the garden of their home at 1 Wealden View, now 27, Mill Bank, during 1940.

THE WAR MEMORIAL

In common with most parishes after the First World War, Headcorn erected a war memorial. It is sited on the south side of the High Street outside Chequers and was designed by C.H. Stevens Esq., Art Master, of Folkestone who executed the metal work, with the exception of the name plate. The stone work was carved by Messrs Prebble and Spain of Folkestone. It consists of a solid base of Cornish Granite standing on three steps of Yorkshire Stone surmounted by a block of Portland Stone. The four jambs are of polished red granite and the solid cap is of Cornish granite. All the embellishments are of beaten copper. On the front is a handsome plate containing the names of the thirty-seven men from the parish who fell in the Great War. It was the gift of E.A. Richford Esq., of Summer Hill. At the back is a large mural wreath; on the right side is a sailor on ship laying his gun, and on the left a soldier in full kit in the trenches.

An unveiling ceremony was performed by Col. F.S.W. Cornwallis CBE on Sunday 12th July 1920. A service of dedication was conducted by the Rev. C.P. Dale, vicar of Headcorn. It was estimated that at least one thousand people attended the ceremony. After the Second World War a further plaque was added with the names of ten men from the parish who gave their lives in that conflict. On the night of 29th February 1952, at about midnight, the war memorial was shattered by Mr E.A. Lock, hairdresser, of Knowle House. He struck it with his private car, suffering cuts and shock. He had the memorial completely restored, and it was re-dedicated at the Remembrance Day service that year by the Rev. Paul Atkins, vicar of Headcorn.

Each year a Remembrance Day Service is still held at the memorial.

The unveiling of the War Memorial by Col. Cornwallis, July 1920.

The morning after the War Memorial was shattered by Mr Lock in February 1952.
(Kent Messenger)

TILDEN

Along the road to Ulcombe lies Tilden Farm. The timber-framed farmhouse is probably fifteenth century in date and has a continuous overhang, or jetty. It contains several interesting features, including a 'smoke shaft', predating the insertion of a chimney stack, and a 'smugglers' wheel', used to haul contraband into the chimney and conceal it from the excisemen in the eighteenth century. There is a local legend of a secret passage leading from Tilden to Moatenden.

Tilden's most famous visitor was William Warham, Archbishop of Canterbury and Chancellor of England, until displaced from the latter post by Cardinal Wolsey in the reign of Henry VIII. His niece, a member of the St Leger family of Ulcombe, lived here and her uncle may have been a frequent guest. His coat of arms in stained glass was formerly in one of the downstairs windows, though it is now to be seen in another farmhouse in the parish.

William Warham, Archbishop of Canterbury 1503-1532.
(By permission of Royal Library, Windsor Castle)

Tilden Farmhouse in the snow, 1986.
(N. Aldridge)

Tilden Farmhouse in 1932 showing the south side with its roundel of stained glass in the window.

Moatenden Farmhouse, 1905.

MOATENDEN

On the north-western outskirts of Headcorn, towards Sutton Valence, lies Moatenden Farm and the site of the former priory of 'Moddenden', which was founded in 1224 by Robert (or Richard) de Rokesley. Sir Robert, the owner of the manor, gave the land to set up one of the first English priories dedicated to the order of Trinitarian Friars. His mother, Margaret de Moddenden, was Abbess of Malling Abbey. Did she give her name to this priory or was it the other way round? Robert Furley in 1878 noted 'Margaret de Modingden . . . the mother of Robert de Rokele' in the patent roll in King John's reign and concludes that the land was named after the lady. Each house of Trinitarians originally had seven friars, the minister, three clerks and three lay brethren; the number was later increased as the priory grew. Although the priory came to own land in Sussex and the Midlands, it was never a rich foundation.

Hard times were experienced in the fourteenth century by the ravages of the Black Death, when the population was decimated. Before that, in 1321, when Leeds Castle was besieged by Edward II, Mottenden suffered greatly. As the army surrounding the castle numbered some 30,000 men they must have plundered the country-side for some miles around to feed themselves, to the detriment of the local populace.

The priory was suppressed at the Dissolution. The few fragments remaining are part of the house still known as 'Moatenden Priory' and consist of a doorway and some windows of fifteenth century date. A large moat still surrounds most of the site. A mill mound is situated some distance away and would have supported a post mill, which would have supplied the priory with flour.

KELSHAM FARM

To the west of the village, near to both the River Beult and the railway line, lies Kelsham, one of the original manor houses of Headcorn. This, and Summer Hill which is nearer the village, were originally one estate and were formerly owned by the Kentish family of Culpeper. It is believed that most of the Bethersden Marble used for building the present parish church was quarried here. The manor later became the home of a family named Kelsham. Although they no longer survive locally, the family has spread worldwide. The writer met a descendant of the family Kelsham-Fullager in 1986. She had travelled from her home in Australia to trace her family history here.

The farmhouse is of considerable architectural interest. The upstairs windows at the front of the house are unusual, while on three sides are blocked mortises — perhaps at one time these were small bay windows. However, these windows do not appear to be original. Inside the house the ceilings are beamed and fairly high. In the roof space it is soon obvious that the north end of the building is later than the southern for most of the rafters are re-used materials. The roof construction in the earlier part is not readily visible, but the former outside end wall of the house is preserved in the roof space, complete with its coating of wattle and daub. The earlier house is probably datable to the late sixteenth or early seventeenth century and the later addition to the late seventeenth century.

Wick Farmhouse, 1920.

Grove House, Wheeler Street, in 1900 showing the original house. At this time it was the home of Mr Potter (second right) uncle to Mr Kingsland. Note the sporty velocipede on the left with its rider.

Grove House, Wheeler Street, about 1911, taken after the earlier house had been enlarged. Mrs Kingsland is inside the front gate with Mrs McKenzie, her sister, outside. Their mother, Mrs Unicume, is at the upstairs window.

Wheeler Street, looking west in 1900. The old Black Horse public house on the left, was demolished about 1920. Tom Longhurst is the man with the cycle. The white house on the right was a shop.

Forge Lane, looking south-east, about 1935. Forge Meadows is now on the right of this view.

William Featherstone, who was born in Headcorn in 1807, was a giant of a man standing 6ft 10ins tall. He emigrated to America when he was 23 years old and walked 840 miles from New York to Chicago after the three month voyage across the Atlantic. He settled at Big Foot Prairie, where he built a log cabin, and when his wife joined him he met her in New York in a covered wagon.

(Thames Television)

Taken in 1916 this photograph shows Sir Robert Laird Borden, a relative of the Burden family, on a visit to his ancestral village. He was Prime Minister of Canada from 1911-1920. Left to right are: Sir Robert Laird Borden, Mr Sydney Burden, Mr Thomas Witherden Burden, Mrs Elizabeth Agnes Burden (seated), Miss Ethel Burden, the Prime Minister's Aide (name unknown) and Sydney Winwood Burden. The photograph was taken in the garden of The Beams, 41 High Street.

Mrs Olive Buckman with her daughters Mabel (left) and Grace on her 90th birthday in 1940.

Mrs Jane Butcher, née Wood, one of Headcorn's oldest residents, pictured in 1945 in her garden at Petite Cottage, Church Walk.

Headcorn Bellringers, by the Oak Tree, 4th April 1907: back row — J. Murrell, Charles Penfold, Edward Blackman, Philip Hodgkin (Captain of Bells), George Jeffery, ? Wood and A. Honess. Front row — William Foord, W. Field, H. Judge, Arthur Thomas Slingsby, Walter Field and Walter Waghorn.

William and Elsie Trowell about 1900. They were the children of William Trowell (1858-1923) and Sarah (1870-1958).

Mr Henry Outhwaite, c1900, son of the first Headmaster of Headcorn School. He was the first pupil-teacher at the school, but did not continue teaching. He took up a post with the Astronomer Royal at Greenwich. He returned to Willow House, Headcorn, when he retired. His daughter, Mrs Violet Coveney, was a founder member of the Local History Society.

HEADCORN.
QUEEN'S JUBILEE.
TUESDAY, JUNE 21. 1887

THE COMMITTEE ARE GLAD TO BE ABLE TO ANNOUNCE THE FOLLOWING ARRANGEMENTS :—

UNITED SERVICE OF THANKS-GIVING at the PARISH CHURCH at 3.30 p.m.

Special Service and Hymns, with Short Address.

TEA for all Parishioners over fifty years of age.

This Tea will be held in the PARISH CHURCH SCHOOLROOM. TICKETS of Invitation can be obtained on application to any of the following :—

The VICAR, The Vicarage.	Mr. ELLIS, Waterman's Quarter.
Rev. R. A. ANDREWS, The Village.	Mr. E. CHANTLER, Southernden.
Rev. G. W. WILKINSON, Maidstone Road.	Mr. T. OYLER, Hawkenbury.
Mr. PAIGE, The Post Office.	Mr. JOY, East End.
Mr. STUART, Shenley House.	Mr. GIBSON, Stone Style.
Mr. G. OYLER, Great Tong.	Mr. T. L. BURDEN, Black Mill.

TEA for all Children attending the parish week-day and Sunday schools.

TICKETS will be issued through the Superintendents. Children should bring their own Mugs. This Tea will be held in the CRICKET GROUND, and will be followed by SPORTS and GAMES.

GOD SAVE THE QUEEN!

Mr Jack Strickland, who was the village road sweeper for many years. Taken on his retirement 1979.

A poster for Queen Victoria's Golden Jubilee Service of Thanksgiving, followed by tea for all parishioners over fifty, held on Tuesday 21st June 1887.

Queen Victoria's Diamond Jubilee, 1897. The village sports day was held on fields now part of Rushford Close. The Rev. A.C. Scott, Vicar of Headcorn, is seen here winning the Handicap Race. The celebrations were held on 22nd June.

Interior of the Moat Hall, Moat Road. A fascinating picture, truly a glimpse of Edwardian England. Various village entertainments were held here, such as concerts and film shows, often organised by Mr and Mrs Allen, of Ventnor Lodge.

45

Mr George Jeffery with the two engines at the sewage works in Moat Road about 1920. Mr Jeffery worked here from 1906 to 1947, apart from his service career in the First World War.

Harry Judge's Stock Sale, 1915. The photograph is taken looking east from a field next to the railway line, later to become the housing estate 'Orchard Glade'. The rear of Wheeler Street barn is on the left.

The unveiling of the new village sign, which marked the opening of Day's Green on August Bank Holiday, 1951. Lord Cornwallis performed the unveiling ceremony. The weather was typical of an English Bank Holiday!
(Kent Messenger)

46

Group of workmen at Kingslands Corn Store in Wheeler Street in 1910. This building now belongs to C. Foreman and Sons and is known as 'Foreman's Emporium' (1987). Left to right are: Mr Kingsland, Mr Jack Page and Mr Charles Kingsland Jnr — other not known.

'Three in a Tub', Laurence Woodcock, Sydney Aldridge and Arthur Taylor in 1930.

Floods on the Moat Road between Stephens Bridge and Summer Hill on 27th December 1985. Miss Joselyn Lock is in the foreground. (N. Aldridge)

Herman Paine and his son John haymaking in 1954.

Headcorn village centre.

Parish of Headcorn.

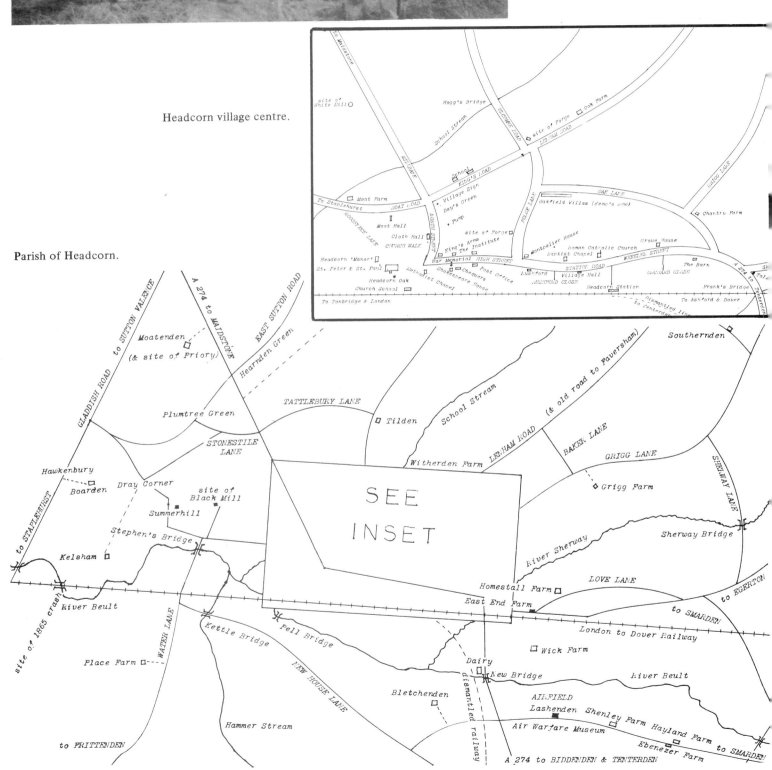

SEE INSET